WILDLIFE
OF NEW ZEALAND
PHOTOGRAPHY BY ROB SUISTED
TEXT BY MATT TURNER

NEW
HOLLAND

CONTENTS

INTRODUCTION

Long isolation from other land masses has left the stamp of individuality on our native plant and animal species, a minority of which have lived here for over 85 million years. It was around then that New Zealand parted from Gondwana, the ancient southern supercontinent, carrying not only dinosaurs but also the ancestral forms of our modern-day tuatara, skinks and frogs, along with many invertebrates. Many more of our native species originated elsewhere: over the millennia they have rafted, swum or blown in from Australia or neighbouring Pacific islands. Some origins remain hazy: for instance, our podocarps – a distinctive group of conifers – are usually thought of as Gondwanan, but they may have arrived later. The jury is also out on the kiwi.

With the land left largely to itself for millions of years, a unique flora and fauna emerged. Of some 245 bird species present at the point of human contact, over 70 per cent were endemic, as were all of the lizards, along with more than 84 per cent of the seed-bearing plants. There were odd gaps: snakes never made it here, and there are only two land mammals, a couple of bat species. We once had a giant crocodile, but it has gone.

Isolation allowed New Zealand's animals to take on physical adaptations or to occupy ecological niches that, in other parts of the world, wouldn't have been feasible because of predatory pressure. Our national bird, the kiwi, is a ground-dwelling, nocturnal grub-eater. Our giant weta, an insect of fantastical size, is another flightless creature of the night: its niche could be compared to that of a mouse.

Later, the spread of introduced dogs, cats, rats, weasels and stoats exposed these natives to new predators or competitors against which they have no defence, and their populations declined alarmingly, many – such as tuatara and spotted kiwi – vanishing from the mainland. The flightless kakapo, a chronically slow breeder like so many of our natives, stood little chance.

For more than a century, conservationists have worked to rid New Zealand's offshore islands of introduced pests and reserve them as strongholds for threatened species. The growing success, too, of protected enclosures, such as Zealandia in Wellington or Maungatautari Ecological Island in the Waikato, offers pockets of safe mainland habitat. Other projects help communities restore, and live in balance with, the native ecosystem.

Left: New Zealand's national bird, the kiwi, forages at night, probing the ground with its bill for earthworms and grubs. Local communities nationwide are working to preserve them.

FOREST

FOREST

Before clearance by human settlers, more than four-fifths of New Zealand's land surface was forested. Southern beech still dominates the South Island, with evergreen rainforest along the wet western seaboard and in the subtropical north. Many of the great trees have gone, but here and there pockets remain, such as at Whirinaki south-east of Rotorua, with its mature podocarps, or Waipoua in Northland, which is home to giant kauri. The forests are a haven for bird life – from secretive kiwi, bellbird and kokako to the more profuse tui, kereru/pigeon, silvereye and fantail. If it's diversity you're after, just bend down and pick through the leaf litter: here there are uncounted fungi and invertebrates, and you may even find a species new to science.

Left: Much of the South Island's native forest is home to southern beech, of which New Zealand has four species – red, hard, mountain, silver – and one subspecies, black. Beech forest supports a rich web of invertebrates and bird life.

Above: New Zealand is a hot spot for ferns, which are found in every habitat and corner of the country and number more than 200 species. Black tree ferns/ mamaku may reach 20 metres tall, with a crown spreading over four metres or more.

Left: The world's heaviest parrot, and one of its rarest, the kakapo is an example of the gigantism and flightlessness that can evolve among long-isolated island birds.

Right: Closely related to the alpine kea, the kaka is a large forest parrot. Despite the lethal-looking bill it is largely vegetarian, though grubs are on the menu.

Below: New Zealand robins are now scarce in the North Island, but are a feature of many of the southern Great Walks, where they search the leaf litter for insects.

Below right: The tui uses a brush-tipped tongue to lap up nectar from flax, kowhai and other flowers. Its song is a swooping medley of glottal clucks and wheezes.

Left: Found on all three main islands, rimu is most populous on the rainy West Coast of the South Island. Known to settlers as 'red pine', it fast became the construction timber of choice.

Above: The New Zealand pigeon/kereru can be surprisingly hard to spot at rest; you're more likely to track it by the whooshing of its powerful wingbeat.

Right: One of the world's largest and longest-lived trees, kauri is a conifer native to the warm north. The massive trunk can attain well over four metres in diameter, and the oldest kauri recorded may have exceeded 2000 years.

Left: The kiwi has a sensory organ at the tip of its bill that picks up the vibrations of prey moving underground.

Above: It's well worth making a dawn visit to a wildlife sanctuary for a chance to hear the kokako, one of the finest singers of any New Zealand bird.

Right: Spreading its tail feathers at brief stationary moments, the fantail often shadows walkers along trails, snapping up insects in their wake.

Left: Kowhai blooms from late winter into spring, attracting tui and bellbirds to its nectar.

Below: Manuka is one of the first native shrubs to recolonise burnt or cleared land. Large pink or white flowers are borne singly; the similar kanuka has clusters of smaller flowers.

Right: The handsome nikau palm is found from the top of the north to Banks Peninsula in the South Island. The massive, spoon-shaped bases of the fronds form a distinctive swollen crownshaft at the top of the trunk. After flowering, the palm produces slow-ripening berries, which attract kereru/New Zealand pigeons.

Above: An ancient insect related to grasshoppers, the weta is heavily armoured and flightless. New Zealand hosts around 100 species, found in various habitats from caves to trees; some, like this Cook Strait giant weta, measure over 70 mm in length, although predation by rats and stoats has left these large individuals scarce today.

Right: Island gigantism has yielded some startlingly large invertebrates. Clockwise from top left: puriri moths, with a wingspan up to 150 mm; stick insect (length up to 110 mm); native giant centipede (150 mm, with a bite to match its size); kauri snail (80 mm across the shell, shown here empty).

Left: New Zealand is home to over 90 species of endemic gecko and skink. This is the ornate skink, a secretive species widespread in the North Island.

Below: The huhu beetle measures up to 50 mm long. Its fat, creamy white grub, considered a delicacy by early Maori, is larger still.

Left: Part worm, part arthropod, the peripatus or velvet worm is an oddity that has changed little in half a billion years. Restricted to damp habitats, it is an active predator on other invertebrates. The New Zealand forest is home to several species, the largest reaching around 35 mm long.

Above: Hochstetter's frog is one of four native species, all small (around 40 mm long) and restricted in range. Distinctly primitive, they have little toe webbing, they don't croak, and the tadpoles forgo an aquatic stage – instead, they develop within the egg before riding on the father's back until grown.

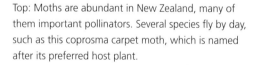

Top: Moths are abundant in New Zealand, many of them important pollinators. Several species fly by day, such as this coprosma carpet moth, which is named after its preferred host plant.

Above: Summer brings the loud chorus of male cicadas calling for a mate. The larvae live in the soil for a few years before clambering out and shedding their skin for adulthood.

Above: With bold wings spanning up to 40 mm, the magpie moth is easy to spot, and it flies by day, too. The adult, like its hairy caterpillar, is distasteful to would-be predators.

Below: Native micro snail on flax.

Bottom: Red admiral butterfly/kahukura on hebe. This beautiful native butterfly lays its eggs on nettle plants.

Right: Glowworm larvae (top) attract prey – in this case, a mayfly – by lowering a sticky thread and 'switching on' their light-emitting organ. Lining the ceilings of many caves, they are a major tourist attraction. The mayfly is New Zealand's most ancient living insect and one of its most ephemeral: the adult lives for just one day.

Left: Measuring up to 18 mm long, the reticulate stag beetle is one of about 25 native New Zealand stag beetle species. It lives in rotten forest timbers.

Below: New Zealand's two species of tuatara are the lone survivors of an ancient group, the Rhynchocephalia, whose heyday was over 200 million years ago. Formerly widespread in mainland forests, today they are confined to offshore islands and protected areas.

Above: Geckos are distinguished from skinks by their granular, rather than smooth, skin. They also cannot blink, hence their use of the tongue in cleaning the eyeballs.

Right: This image of the black tunnelweb spider was used to help create Shelob, the spider in Peter Jackson's *Lord of the Rings: The Return of the King* movie.

SHORE

SHORE

New Zealand's coastline, longer than that of the continental United States, is defined by diversity, combining rocky headlands and peninsulas, deep-watered fiords, bush-fringed coves, mudflats and spits, mangroves and immense sand-dune complexes. Shorebirds, both migrant and resident, flock seasonally on tidal flats at Kaipara, the Firth of Thames, Manawatu and Farewell Spit. Seabirds nest on rock stacks and grassy headlands, penguins using the shoreline undergrowth. Hardy flowering trees and herbs brave the extreme conditions – the alternating deluge, drought, heat and cold – and provide food and habitat for insects from beetles to butterflies. And the mangroves fringing many of the northern estuaries support an intricate web of life involving birds and bees, crustaceans and fish.

Left: Coastal flats at Miranda, on the Firth of Thames south of Auckland. From September, shorebirds will arrive in their thousands from northern hemisphere breeding grounds: these include godwit, red knot, ruddy turnstone, eastern curlew, various sandpipers, and more. New Zealand birds, such as pied oystercatcher and wrybill, join them later from the South Island.

Above left: In spring the New Zealand dotterel takes on its russet-breasted breeding plumage. Nests are simple scrapes in beach sand.

Above right: Wiped from the mainland by cats and rats, the endemic New Zealand shore plover/tuturuatu is found today only on offshore island reserves.

Above left: Pohutukawa rings the coasts of the upper North Island, often fringing the tideline, where it takes a drenching of salt spray. Scarlet blossom draws the birds, bees and even geckos to feed on its nectar and pollen.

Above right: Sprawling over rocks and grassy banks, the white- or pink-flowering ice plant/horokaka is a coastal succulent, storing moisture in its fat, juicy, triangular-section leaves.

Right: Pingao, an endemic species of sedge, spreads by putting out rhizomes, which anchor sand dunes in gentle, aerodynamically stable slopes. It's increasingly rare, due to competition from introduced marram grass.

Left and right: Every year, bar-tailed godwits fly in for the southern summer, flocking on coastal feeding grounds. Come autumn, they depart for their breeding grounds in the Arctic, completing an annual round trip of some 30,000 kilometres.

Below: The Auckland Island shag is one of 14 shag species in the New Zealand region. Shags tend to nest in colonies, either in tree branches by the water or on cliff edges.

Left: The endemic yellow-eyed penguin/hoiho breeds on southern coasts and on offshore islands. It is very rare, threatened by the clearance of the coastal vegetation on which it depends for nesting.

Right: The Fiordland crested penguin/tawaki nests around the shores of Fiordland and Stewart Island, feeding mainly on squid and krill.

Below: Smallest of all the world's penguins, the blue penguin/korora is a common sight off the coast; if you sail out for a spot of fishing you may well see one or two bobbing in the water.

Above: The common copper butterfly (left), which lays its eggs on *Muehlenbeckia*, is frequently sighted on coasts, whereas the katipo (right), a relative of the Australian redback, is an increasingly rare find. It lives among the driftwood and shore vegetation.

Right: Native bees perform a valuable service in New Zealand, pollinating not only native flowers but also food crops. There are 27 species in all; they nest in loose soil and tend to live solo, rather than in colonies.

Left: The mangrove forests that form along northern North Island coasts are surprisingly rich in wildlife, and they also help stabilise the land against storm damage.

Right: White-faced herons are stalk-and-strike hunters, either perching patiently, waiting to spot movement, or wading very slowly through the shallows.

Below: Mangrove trees survive extreme daily ranges in temperature, moisture and salinity; numerous adaptations, including leaves that can secrete salt, enable them to survive inundation by sea water.

MARINE

MARINE

You need not venture far offshore to appreciate the wealth of New Zealand's marine life. At Kaikoura, for instance, the nutrients stirred up from deep ocean trenches nourish the fish and squid sought by dolphins and sperm whales, while above water you may spot 10 to 12 albatross species. By virtue of their isolation, the offshore island groups – the Poor Knights, Kermadecs, Chathams, Snares and Auckland Islands, among others – remain pest-free strongholds for ocean-roaming seabirds and seals, many of which also have toeholds on the mainland coasts. Close in, a network of more than 30 marine reserves protects selected areas from exploitation, while at the same time allowing the public a glimpse, be it through a diving mask or a hull floor, of sea life in the wild.

Left: Rocky coasts around the South Island and the lower North are prime real estate for the New Zealand fur seal, which comes ashore to breed during summer or to rest at other times of the year. On land they have an awkward gait; under water they are gracile and swift.

Above: Female New Zealand sea lion at Nugget Point, Otago; a full-grown bull can reach three times the cow's size. Hunted on the mainland by early Maori, and later by European sealers, the sea lion population is now largely confined to subantarctic islands; a small colony is today trying to regain a toehold in Otago.

This page, clockwise from above: Hector's dolphins cruise off Banks Peninsula (Maui's dolphin, an endemic subspecies of the Hector's found off the North Island, is now critically endangered). Common dolphins can be seen all around our coasts, often bow-riding or alongside boats. The orca or killer whale, New Zealand's largest native dolphin, forages in coastal waters for stingray.

Right: Cook Strait, and the deep trenches that lie off the South Island's Kaikoura coast, are nutrient-rich feeding grounds for sperm whales, which dive to grapple with giant squid.

Left, clockwise from above: Snapper are most numerous in northern coastal waters up to 200 metres deep; they have attractive spots and bars that fade fast when out of the water. Kelpfish are bottom-dwellers, hard to spot on the reef. The goatfish uses its long barbels to stir up small prey from the seabed.

Above: Trevally live in waters up to 100 metres or so deep, often forming huge schools in association with other shoaling fish, and feeding on the surface.

Right: Parore are found from the Cook Strait north, mostly in shallow waters, where they feed on everything from seaweed to crabs and plankton.

Above: The white-capped or shy albatross is one of the smaller albatrosses – small being a relative term for a bird with a wingspan measuring up to 2.6 metres. Breeding on the subantarctic islands, it is often spotted off the coast of Stewart Island, in the wake of fishing vessels.

Opposite, clockwise from top left: The northern giant petrel/pangurunguru eats almost anything – carrion, penguin chicks, fish and squid. Patchy piebald plumage identifies the cape petrel/titore, which ranges into New Zealand waters during winter. Hutton's shearwaters/titi gather to feed.

Left: The southern Buller's albatross/toroa-teoteo breeds on the Snares and Solander islands to the south of New Zealand, building a mounded nest of seaweed and mud. Like the white-capped albatross (page 50), it is seen off Stewart Island.

Above: The main breeding ground of the endemic black petrel/taiko, a burrow nester, is on Great Barrier Island in the Hauraki Gulf.

Right: Diving petrels nest in burrows on offshore islands – here, Mana Island off Wellington.

MOUNTAIN

MOUNTAIN

New Zealand straddles the boundary of the Australian and Pacific plates, and tectonic movement has thrown up the main divide, the long spine that runs roughly north–south from the Central Volcanic Plateau down to Fiordland and finds its highest elevations among the Southern Alps in Westland and Canterbury. In high-elevation zones, which extend from montane (300–1000 metres) to subalpine (600–1500) and alpine (1500+), wildlife is tailored to the testing conditions. Insects may be dark-coloured to absorb warmth, and plants often have a compact growth habit, and/or small leaves, for natural insulation. Our largest buttercup, the Mount Cook lily, lives in the 'now': there are pores on both sides of its leaves, rather than just one, and they open or close at intervals to exploit prevailing sources of warmth.

Left: The endemic Mount Cook lily is not a lily at all, but the world's largest buttercup, with blooms up to 8 cm in diameter and leaves up to 40 cm across. It's a hardy plant, with foliage specially adapted to survive the heat reflected off sun-baked rocks.

Above: Mount Cook lilies adorn Mackinnon Pass, the literal highpoint of the Milford Track in Fiordland. Most of New Zealand's alpine flowers have white petals: their chief pollinators are flies, beetles and moths, which have monochrome vision, rather than bees and butterflies, which see in full colour.

Left: Several species of tussock grass dominate the New Zealand grasslands, especially in alpine zones. Tussocks are hardy plants, thanks to the bunching structure of their stems, which creates a local microclimate protecting much of the plant from the elements.

Above: Alpine hard fern labours under something of a misnomer: it's found at all altitudes from sea level up to 2000 metres, all over New Zealand and beyond, south as far as the subantarctic islands.

Left, clockwise from top: Agile and swift in flight, the New Zealand falcon/karearea hunts in forests and open land for live prey ranging from smaller birds to rabbits. A little bird bobbing up and down on the rocky slopes of a South Island herbfield is likely to be the endemic rock wren. Blue duck/whio are rare inhabitants of mountain streams.

Right: The kea is the world's only alpine parrot, haunting the South Island ranges and peaks. Intelligent and inquisitive, it has no fear of trampers and freely rips into their packs and tents.

Below: Rare today outside protected areas, the takahe is a heavyweight relative of the pukeko.

Left: Brown skua chick in bidi-bidi. At higher, cooler latitudes, alpine plants like these grow at lower altitudes.

Above: *Hebe macrantha* ('large-flowering') is found on alpine and subalpine slopes along the length of the main divide, from Nelson south to Fiordland.

Right: *Dracophyllum menziesii*, popularly called pineapple scrub, forms shrubs up to a metre high at a range of altitudes in the South and Stewart islands.

Left: *Ourisia* is a genus of charming white (and occasionally pink-flushed) flowering herbs found in all three main islands, mostly in the montane to alpine zone.

Below: Two varieties of snowberry, a low-growing shrub, grow at higher altitudes on the North and South islands. The pink or white fruits, once used as a food source by early settlers, appear from January onwards.

Right: In response to the paucity of nutrients in the soil of bogs and alpine meadows, sundews have evolved a carnivorous habit. Hairs on the leaves exude a sticky fluid that traps insects, whose soft parts are then digested by further secretions from the leaves.

Left: Warm sunny days bring the scree skink out to bask on rocks. This rare lizard lives from North Otago to Marlborough at elevations up to 1400 metres.

Above: The mountain giant dragonfly is a large hunter of other insects among high-altitude streams and scrub. Its black-and-yellow body measures up to 80 mm in length.

Right: New Zealand's grasshoppers come in an endless variety of colours and markings. Those at high altitudes tend to be dark, an adaptation that helps them absorb precious heat.

WETLAND

WETLAND

Wetlands include coastal estuaries and lagoons, as well as inland rivers, lakes, swamps and marshes. Many of our iconic plants, among them kahikatea and raupo, thrive on having wet feet. Though land reclamation has destroyed over 90 per cent of New Zealand's wetlands, they remain valuable habitats for birds and other wildlife. And though our native freshwater fish receive less attention than the exotic sport fish, they total more than 40 species; almost all are endemic, and a great many – the longfin eel is a standout example – spend part of their life cycle at sea. On a smaller scale we have invertebrates, such as the mayflies and caddisflies, that date from Gondwanan origins.

Left and right: Found in every region except
Southland, raupo grows deep and thick on the
margins of swamps, spreading by means of its
underwater rhizomes. The straplike leaves can reach a
towering three metres in height, and the female (fat,
brown) part of the flower head, a staple food source
for early Maori, measures up to 30 cm long. Raupo is
a valuable habitat for wetland birds.

Below: A worldwide bird, the white heron/kotuku
breeds in only one New Zealand location: the
Waitangiroto River at Okarito, Westland. Outside
the breeding season it frequents rivers and wetlands
around the country.

Above left: Some 170 species of sedge are native to New Zealand, lining the channels of saltmarshes and freshwater creeks. This is jointed wire rush/oioi, which reaches a metre in height and provides habitat for the fernbird/matata.

Above right: Despite its bright plumage, the New Zealand kingfisher/kotare can be hard to spot until it flies from one perch to the next. Common in wetlands and on shores, it hunts for fish and invertebrates, diving on them in shallows and among vegetation.

Right: It's as common to see New Zealand flax/harakeke lining a motorway as fringing a lake, but it thrives in wetlands, offering birds protective habitat and a food source in the form of the flowers on its long, zigzag stems.

Left: Kahikatea, here lining Lake Wahapo in Westland, once formed large forests in swampy areas, but it has declined in the wake of drainage and felling for timber.

Above left: The exuvia, or casing, of a giant dragonfly nymph. The nymph lives for several years in a mud burrow, preying on smaller creatures and moulting occasionally until ready to make the final change.

Above right: Damselflies mating.

Right: The New Zealand dabchick/weweia is a smallish species of grebe found only in the North Island. Spending most of its life on the water, it is an adept diver, able to stay submerged for 10 to 25 seconds.

Left: The inanga is one of five *Galaxias* species collectively known as whitebait; the juvenile fish are netted as they swim upstream after developing at sea.

Below left: Short-jawed kokopu, a widespread fish up to 300 mm in length.

Below: Longfin eels undergo a remarkable life cycle. Adults head for the ocean, near Tonga, to spawn, and then die. Their larvae eventually return to New Zealand, where they may grow for up to a century before making their own one-way breeding voyage.

Right: Freshwater crayfish/koura play a key ecological role in our wetlands by scavenging organic matter, such as old leaves and dead invertebrates. As such, their presence indicates that the water is healthy.

Left: Royal spoonbills are a relatively new arrival in New Zealand, settling from Australia in the 1940s. Serrated margins to the bill help the bird filter food particles from water.

Above: No New Zealand wetland, from coastal swamp to city park, is complete without pukeko. They nest in thickets and feed on all sorts, from roots and shoots to fish, insects, carrion and other birds' eggs.

Right: Brown teal/pateke tend to lie low by day, emerging to feed at dawn and dusk. They are rare today, with the main population on Great Barrier Island and smaller pockets in Northland and Fiordland.

Also available from Rob Suisted and New Holland

978 1 86966 333 9

978 1 86966 415 2

978 1 86966 416 9

978 1 86966 376 6

978 1 86966 332 2

978 1 86966 377 3

First published in 2013 by New Holland Publishers (NZ) Ltd
Auckland • Sydney • London

www.newhollandpublishers.co.nz

218 Lake Road, Northcote, Auckland 0627, New Zealand
Unit 1, 66 Gibbes Street, Chatswood, NSW 2067, Australia
The Chandlery, Unit 114, 50 Westminster Bridge Road,
London, SE1 7QY, United Kingdom

Copyright © 2013 in photography: Rob Suisted,
    www.naturespic.com
Copyright © 2013 New Holland Publishers (NZ) Ltd

Publishing manager: Christine Thomson
Writer: Matt Turner
Editor: Brian O'Flaherty
Design: Trevor Newman

Front cover: Tuatara
Title page: Ornate skink
Contents page: Hector's dolphins in Flea Bay, Banks Peninsula

Pages 4–5: Herons, shags and gulls feeding on tidal
mudflats behind Boulder Bank, Nelson
Back cover, from top to bottom: Red admiral butterfly on
hebe; New Zealand falcon/karearea; New Zealand snapper

A catalogue record for this book is available from the
National Library of New Zealand.

ISBN: 978 1 86966 400 8

Colour reproduction by Pica Digital Pte Ltd, Singapore
Printed in China at Everbest Printing Co, on paper sourced
from sustainable forests.

10 9 8 7 6 5 4 3 2